Memoirs of a Loughborough Man

A.E. Shepherd
1872 - 1962

Edited by

Joy Cross and Margaret Staple

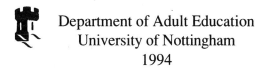

Department of Adult Education
University of Nottingham
1994

Centre for Local History Record Series no. 9

First published in 1994 by
The Department of Adult Education
Education Building
University Park, Nottingham NG7 2RD

© Department of Adult Education
University of Nottingham

ISBN   1 85041 076 3

Printed by Technical Print Services Ltd, Brentcliffe Avenue,
Carlton Road, Nottingham NG3 7AG

MEMOIRS OF A LOUGHBOROUGH MAN

A.E. SHEPHERD
1872 - 1962

Shepherd Family Tree

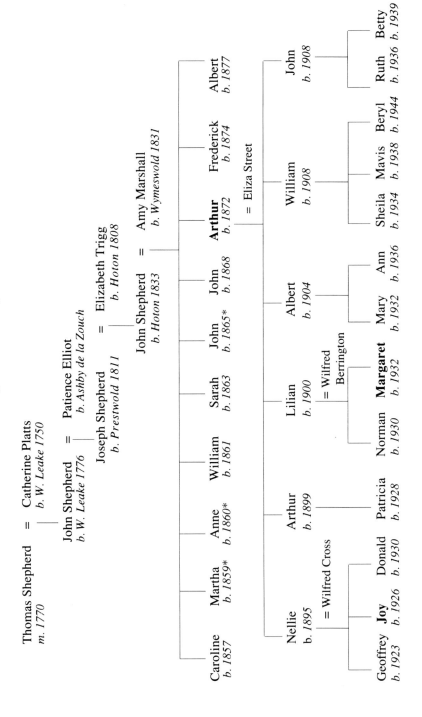

Thomas Shepherd = Catherine Platts
m. 1770   *b. W. Leake 1750*

John Shepherd = Patience Elliot
b. W. Leake 1776   *b. Ashby de la Zouch*

Joseph Shepherd = Elizabeth Trigg
b. Prestwold 1811   *b. Hoton 1808*

John Shepherd = Amy Marshall
b. Hoton 1833   *b. Wymeswold 1831*

Caroline *b. 1857*

Martha *b. 1859**

Anne *b. 1860**

William *b. 1861*

Sarah *b. 1863*

John *b. 1865**

John *b. 1868*

Arthur *b. 1872* = Eliza Street

Frederick *b. 1874*

Albert *b. 1877*

Nellie *b. 1895* = Wilfred Cross

Arthur *b. 1899*

Lilian *b. 1900* = Wilfred Berrington

Albert *b. 1904*

William *b. 1908*

John *b. 1908*

Geoffrey *b. 1923*

Joy *b. 1926*

Donald *b. 1930*

Patricia *b. 1928*

Norman *b. 1930*

Margaret *b. 1932*

Mary *b. 1932*

Ann *b. 1936*

Sheila *b. 1934*

Mavis *b. 1938*

Beryl *b. 1944*

Ruth *b. 1936*

Betty *b. 1939*

* died same day

CONTENTS

List of illustrations   vi

Foreword   vii

Preface   ix

Chapter 1   1872-1882 Early Years   1

Chapter 2   1883-1892 Work and Leisure   9

Chapter 3   1893-1913 Business and Family Man   21

Chapter 4   1914-1918 The Great War   32

Chapter 5   1918-1939 Property Development   37

Chapter 6   1939 - 1952 War and its Aftermath   44

LIST OF ILLUSTRATIONS

Cover: Arthur Shepherd at 'Charnwood', c. 1923.

Frontispiece: The Shepherd Family Tree.

1. The November Fair, c. 1910.   4

2. Map of Loughborough in the Early 20th Century.   8

3. The Shepherd Family, c. 1898.   20

4. Arthur Shepherd, 1896.   22

5. The Shepherd's Shop in Nottingham Road, 1901.   28

6. Robin's Breakfast, c. 1920.   31

7. Arthur Shepherd and Family, 1916.   34

8. Army Assembles in the Market Place, 1914.   35

9. Proposed Street Widening in Loughborough, 1923.   40

10. Arthur and Eliza Shepherd on their Golden   45
    Wedding Anniversary, 1944.

Illustrations 1, 2, 5 and 9 have been reproduced from *Bygone Loughborough in Photographs* (1973), by kind permission of the Leicestershire Libraries and Information Service.

The cover photograph and illustrations 3, 4, 6, 7, 8 and 10 are from the Shepherd family collection.

FOREWORD

This autobiography of my grandfather, A.E. Shepherd of Loughborough, Leicestershire, 1872-1962, was compiled, edited and transcribed from jottings he made in little notebooks and on old sheets of paper, and from dictated notes and conversations we had during the summer of 1951. It began while he was in hospital recovering from a serious fracture of his thigh and continued throughout the summer, often in the garden at 'Highcroft' while he impatiently endured enforced inactivity. His consultant orthopaedic surgeon had told him there was little likelihood that he would ever be able to walk again. He did not know my grandfather, who persisted doggedly until he could walk again, albeit awkwardly and with a stick. He resumed driving his car (to the peril of all!), built a bungalow on land adjoining 'Highcroft' so that he could still enjoy the sight of 'his' rhododendron bushes and roses in the garden next door, and lived, with my grandmother for another ten years.

Margaret L. Staple (née Berrington)

For the purposes of this book a further editing was necessary, omitting information that did not refer to the Loughborough area. Grandfather took a knowledgeable interest in national events but he was essentially a Loughborough man.

I am indebted to the Leicester Libraries and Information Service for the permission to reproduce several photographs from *Bygone Loughborough in Photographs*. Every effort has been made to trace the copyright holders.

Joy Cross

Joy Cross, the daughter of Arthur Shepherd's eldest daughter Nellie, spent her early life in Loughborough and Nottingham. A history graduate of London University, she taught history at Wisbeach High School and Bournmouth School for Girls. Her other publications include *Imagery in the Churches of Nottinghamshire, Derbyshire and Leicestershire*, Department of Adult Education, University of Nottingham (1991), and *Prestwold Hall to Branksome Tower. C.W. Packe 1792-1867*, Bournmouth Local Studies Publications (1993).

Margaret Staple is the daughter of Arthur Shepherd's daughter Lilian. She is a history graduate of London University and taught at various schools including Cardiff Girls High School and Park High School, Stanmore, Harrow.

Also available in the Local History Record Series

Diaries of Henry Hill of Slackfields Farm, 1872-1896
Edited by J. Heath

Life at Laxton 1800-1903: The Childhood Memories of Edith Hickson
Edited by B. A. Wood, C. Watkins, and C. A. Wood

Religion in Victorian Nottinghamshire: The Religious Census of 1851 (two volumes)
Edited by Michael Watts

The Local Historian's Glossary and Vade Mecum 2nd Edition
Compiled by Joy Bristow

Forthcoming 1994

Sounding Boards: Oral Testimony and the Local Historian
David Marcombe

PREFACE

Arthur Shepherd's memoirs provide a fascinating account of Loughborough between the late Victorian years and the second World War. His is a story of considerable social mobility — a classic tale of the boy from a humble beginning who later owns the big house he earlier had admired. It is also a rare account of property developing in a small town.

Shepherd's reminiscences touch on many of the more colourful aspects of Loughborough's history. He not only saw but played on Great Paul, the nearly seventeen-ton bell cast by Taylor's Bell Foundry for St. Paul's Cathedral and moved to London by traction engine one week in May 1887. He admired Loughborough's football team, which in the 1890's briefly played in the Second Division. He witnessed the Zeppelin raid of 31 January 1916, during which six people were killed.

Yet the fascination of his account lies in his description of the more ordinary aspects of Loughborough, especially when he was young. His account of his struggles with a barrow on the old roads, the Friendly Society parades, the suffering during the major industrial disputes and hardship from the severe winter of early 1895 are all notably memorable.

Arthur Shepherd pays testimony to Alderman Clemerson who helped him to success early in this trade. The firm of Clemersons had grown since its foundation as an ironmongers in 1848, expanding into a departmental store in 1887. Later Henry Clemerson may even have encouraged Shepherd to stand for the council. Shepherd's retirement from local politics after ten years as a Liberal councillor, though primarily to do with his growing property activities and the possible clash of interest with his council role, may well have owed something to the markedly less favourable political conditions for him at the end of the First World War.

In 1919 the old struggles between Tory and Liberal were overshadowed by the arrival of a challenge from Labour. Before 1914 no Labour councillors had been elected to Loughborough Council. In 1919 and 1920 Labour won a high proportion of those seats which came up for the annual election. Indeed counting by-elections as well, Labour won 9 out of 14 contests. The Liberals were wiped out for over a decade. Not until the 1930s was a Liberal candidate standing as a 'straight' Liberal (as opposed to Independent Labour candidate) elected to Loughborough borough council.

Moreover, others Shepherd had worked with left the council after the war. The Conservatives and Liberals soon worked together in the face of the Labour challenge. Nevertheless, in 1919 one of two Conservative councillors lost in Hastings Ward and in 1920 both did, with Henry Clemerson coming bottom of the poll with 688 votes, to the victorious Labour candidates' votes of 982 and 876. It is likely that Shepherd's interest in contesting again a seat for the council would have diminished with the departure of his friend and mentor.

Those interested in Loughborough's history can only be delighted that Arthur Shepherd's recollections were recorded and that Joy Cross and Margaret Staple have edited them. They are an enjoyable addition to Loughborough's history.

Professor Christopher Wrigley, Nottingham, 1994

Christopher Wrigley is Professor of Modern British History at Nottingham University. He is a former borough and county councillor as well as a past Parliamentary candidate for Loughborough.

Chapter 1

1872 - 1882
Early Years

I was born on March 16th 1872 of very humble and God-fearing parents in a small house in Freehold Street, belonging to the late Mr. John Taylor, the Bell Founder. My father and mother lived there for over fifty years. The rent when they first went there being 2/8d. per week, inclusive, afterwards being raised to 3/2d. per week. They brought up their family of five boys and two girls. My eldest sister Caroline was in service and my other sister Sally used to sleep at the neighbour's house next door.

My father was a tailor and he had to work very hard from morning till night. He never earned much money and my parents had a great struggle to make both ends meet. Although poor we always had plenty of plain good wholesome food. My mother was a very good cook and was able to make the best of very little. We owed a great deal to our parents for the way we were brought up. We were never allowed to stay away from school and always had to attend Sunday School, both morning and afternoon. Every Sunday night my mother used to gather all her children together and offer up a prayer on our behalf, asking God to watch over us and pray that we might grow up good Christians and useful citizens.

The earliest recollection of my childhood was drinking out of a teapot which stood on the hob and scalding myself. I was only 2½ years old at the time. The next thing I remember was being sent to an old Dame School across the road. I was not much more than 3 years old. I did not learn very much; I think I was only sent to be out of the way of my mother.

At the age of six I went to the old Church Gate School. The schoolmaster was named Scholfield. He was very fond of using the cane. In fact it was thought the only way to instil learning into a boy. I do not remember much about the schooling there. I remember that Mr. Wallace Adcock was a monitor and Mr. J. James came while I was there. He afterwards went to the Loughborough Grammar School and stayed there until his retirement.

Two amusing incidents occurred; a boy was sent to look after our class (which was in the classroom adjoining the main room), because the teacher had not come that morning, and while the headmaster was away from the main room another of the boys in the top class came into our classroom and started to chase the boy who was looking after us round the room. While this was going on the headmaster came in and wanted to know what all the commotion was about. Of course the boy who was sent to look after us made his case good, but the master took the other boy, laid him across the desk, turned his trousers down and gave him several strokes on his bare bottom with the cane.

The other incident was when some boys had asked to leave the room, and once outside began to play on the swings in the yard. The master came out and as the swing came down he cut the boys with his cane. This was more than the boys could stand for any length of time so they climbed up the swing and sat astride the top rail, refusing to come down. The master waited below like a cat watching a mouse.

When I was seven I was sent to the Board School which was in an old disused factory in Pinfold Gate passage. It stood on the site of the present Cobden Infant School. At the entrance was the town's pinfold where stray cattle were put. I have seen several different sorts of animals enclosed there until their owners came to claim them. Mr. Henry Kelsey was the headmaster, and although fond of the cane he was an excellent teacher. I think Mr. Kelsey and to a lesser extent Mr. Upton and

Mr. Judges turned out more businessmen for the town than any other masters. A few years ago there was a reunion of old Cobden Street boys. These included Mr. Chas Moss, Mr. Alan Moss, Mr. Simpson the plumber, Mr. George Attenborough and many other well known businessmen of the town.

We had to pay 2d. each per week as a school fee, and as there were three of us this meant that my parents had to find 6d. a week, which was a considerable item in those days. I spent four happy years at Cobden Street School. Perhaps the cane was used a little more freely than was necessary — I know I had my fair share, very often when I didn't deserve it, although sometimes I missed it when I did deserve it, so perhaps it evened itself out. I remember a particular incident when I was in the fifth standard. We were given five sums to do. Mr. Kelsey told us that he would give any boy one stroke of the cane for every sum he got wrong. One boy, who later became a well known businessman, got three sums wrong. Having received a stroke on each hand, the boy was told to hold out his hand again, which he refused to do. He was brought to the front of the class and asked again 'hold out your hand'. Again the boy said 'shan't', whereupon the master struck him with the cane and the boy swore and went for the master and a freefight ensued, from which I can assure you the master came off second best. The boy's elder brother was also in the class and a letter was written for him to take home to his father. The boy was told that if he held out his hand the letter would not be sent. This time he obeyed and thus ended a fight which kept the class amused for a good half hour. There was little more work done that morning.

We children got most of our entertainment from our Sunday School. The teachers of most churches took a very active part in providing entertainment for the children attending their schools. Of course the great attraction of the year was the November Fair. I think the fair was more attractive then. Today

1. The November Fair, c. 1910.

it has become more mechanical and has a large number of gambling machines. The shows in the past had very elaborate gilded fronts with very fine and expensive organs. The Cattle Fair was one of the largest in the country. It was held on a Thursday and occupied the main streets of the town. The horses were paraded and sold in Wards End. There used to be droves of Welsh mountain ponies and some very good bargains to be had. I have seen droves of geese being driven into market for sale. The drovers used to collect them at different farms as they came along.

During the Cattle Fair most of the shops used to be boarded up to prevent them from being damaged, although the windows at that time were mostly small panes. At the time of writing I know of only one of these windows still remaining and that is at the corner of Bedford Place and Albert Street. Eventually the fair was moved to a recreation ground where Ratcliffe Road and Burder Street stand. Friday was the 'statitts' when the hiring of farm servants took place; those who were hired bound themselves for one year and by law they had to serve that time. I remember that on Statitts Day it was almost impossible to push one's way through the crowds of servants and farmers at the bottom of the market. Hiring was generally clinched by a gift according to the generosity of the farmer which was not generally of a very high standard. However, the amount received did not affect the holiday spirit and the remainder of the day was given over to pleasure.

There was another fair in the summer, but it was not so large nor so popular. It was called Holy Thursday or White Apron Fair. You could see the farmer's wife come with poultry, eggs, cheeses and butter for sale. Eggs at that time sold at about sixteen a shilling.

For the rest of the year we children made our own amusement. The streets were our playground, and there were no fears of being run over unless a horse took fright and ran away, which seldom happened. Occasionally some Italian would come round with a large brown bear which danced for us. The man had a long pole which he tossed in the air and the bear had to catch it. There were also performing cats and birds.

Two events in particular stand out in my memory. One was the celebration of Robert Raikes' centenary in 1880 when all the scholars of the Sunday Schools met in the Market Place and sang hymns to celebrate the first opening of a Sunday School for children. I well remember one of the hymns, the first verse ran something like this:

> *'A hundred summers have passed away since one knelt down and cried and opened the doors of a Sunday School to welcome a little child.'*

The other event was the casting of the large bell, 'Great Paul', for St. Paul's Cathedral, London. This bell weighed over 17 tons and was cast by John Taylor and Son at the Freehold St. Foundry. After it was cast it was raised on blocks about eighteen inches from the ground in the casting shop, for exhibition. People from all over the district came to see it and when it was struck by the clapper it could be heard miles away. I was very young and we boys used to get under it and swing on the clapper. I remember one Saturday morning when a large party of ladies and gentlemen were on a visit to see it. I was swinging on the clapper when one boy pushed me a bit too far and the clapper struck the bell. The people rushed to get out of the building wondering what had happened. We also rushed away with Mr. Taylor after us. Fortunately we were not caught, but after that no boys were allowed in the building. This bell was taken by road to London, drawn by a traction engine, with a man walking in front with a red flag as the law demanded. No mechanical vehicle was allowed to go faster than three miles per hour, so it took several days to reach its destination. When it started off all the children at Cobden Street School were allowed out to see it go by, and there were reports in the daily papers each day giving its progress. As most transport was horse drawn, you can imagine that a traction engine pulling such a load was a source of great excitement to us.

I have mentioned that my parents had a very hard struggle to bring us up. To help out, my brother and I used to chop firewood at night, after school. Then on Friday night and Saturday morning, we went round to sell it at 2d. a basketful. By this means we were able to earn between us about six or seven shillings a week, which was a great help to our family exchequer. Although poor, my parents always saw that we were well fed. Father had an allotment which he cultivated; also a couple of pigs were kept in a sty at the bottom of the garden. We had plenty of fat bacon to eat, as father never reckoned to kill them until they reached over twenty score lbs. in weight. The killing of the pig in late Autumn was a great event. Then we had pork pie and sausages. We were busy making and sending them to our aunts and uncles who were farmers at Wymeswold. Later we would have a pie come back to our home when they killed their pig.

These were jolly times for we children. Sunday morning was the great day for cutting up the pie and we used to watch with longing eyes the marking out in equal parts, and there were mince pies later in the day and during the week. As tea at that time was very dear, we always had to have a basin of bread and milk for breakfast. I was sent up to a house on Forest Road belonging to the late Mr. Gilbert Tucker who kept a few cows and I used to get a half gallon of very good skimmed milk for 2d. I used to think what a wonderful house it was with its trees and flower gardens, little thinking that some day I should become the owner.

In 1882 the town was very small compared with what it is today. There were several passages which ran through the town. One started in Meadow Lane, went up Duke Street by the Star Foundry, along the Coneries into Baxter Gate; a branch went off into Craddock Street, Pinfold Jetty on to Wellington Street, Moira Street and so on to Factory Street, Queen Street and Leicester Road. Another passage went from Park Road along Royland Road by the Blacksmith Arms, Browns Lane onto Ashby Road and Garendon Lane. I must not forget the many courts and alleys, some of which remain today. As I shall relate later, I was apprenticed to the painting and decorating trade, so I became acquainted with these courts and alleys through having worked in most of them. I can give a fair account of the number of houses in these courts. Church Gate had about twenty, Nottingham Road thirty, Steeple Row twenty, Baxter

Gate about forty. There were others in Sparrow Hill, Pinfold Gate, High Street, Market Place, Mills Yard, Wards End etc. All told some three hundred houses most of which have been destroyed.

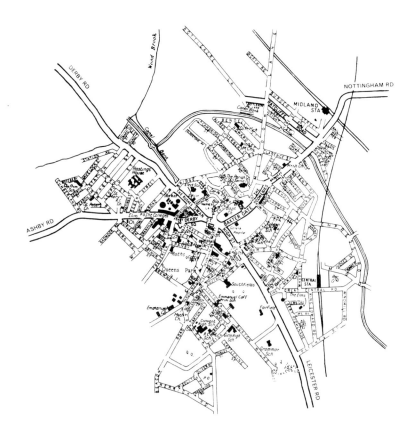

2. The extent of Loughborough in the early 20th century. Based on Ordnance Survey mapping with permission of the controller of HMSO.

Chapter 2

1883 - 1892
Work and Leisure

In October 1883 I finished school, having passed into the sixth standard. This made me eligible to leave school although I was only eleven years six months old. I started full time work at the Co-operative Society, Woodgate. I had to be there at 6 a.m. to assist the baker with the bread. After the bread was put into the oven and until it was ready to be drawn out, I was found work in the front shop, such as cleaning windows, grinding coffee beans, or chopping lump sugar into the required size. The sugar came in blocks about the size and shape of acetylene cylinders.

When the bread was baked I went back to the bakehouse to help there. Then I loaded my handcart with bread and groceries ready for delivery round the town. I used to deliver about 20 stone of bread per day together with parcels of groceries, etc. This used to take me till about six or seven o'clock at night. Then my day's work was finished. I would point out there was no steam roller in the town at that time, and when they mended the roads loose stones were put on roughly and the carts had to crush them down. Many were the times when I was simply stuck and unable to move until some kind friend, seeing my helpless condition came and gave me a helping hand. I was never afraid of hard work, but on looking back I sometimes wonder how I managed to pull through.

For this job I received the princely sum of six shillings a week. I endured three years of this hard labour and shall always look back upon it with horror as the worst three years of my life. During this time the front shop was burnt out, with all the stock.

Two days afterwards the manager confessed to setting it on fire. He was tried at Leicester Assizes and sentenced to five years' imprisonment. He was a very nice man but got very depressed because business was not good. A petition was raised for his release — I used to go round at night to collect signatures, and after being in prison for nine months the Home Secretary pardoned him and he came back to work at the shop. But business became very bad, the baker gave notice of leaving and the Committee wondered if the baking and grocery business could be combined. I was now 13 years of age and had been there 2½ years. The Committee asked if I could manage to do the baking with the help of the new manager until he got used to it. I was willing to try and they raised my wages to ten shillings per week. It was terribly hard work and I had to work all through Friday night to get Saturday's bread out. We didn't get on very well together as he objected to taking any suggestions from me. I had now been there three years, and one week I received quite suddenly a week's notice from the Committee.

My father went to the Committee to find out the reason for my notice but he could get no satisfaction and to this day I do not know why I was stopped. Thus ended three years of what I always look upon as years of slavery.

I immediately got another job with Messrs. B. Clemerson and Son and in comparison it was like being in heaven. The hours were still long, going at 8 a.m. and finishing at 8 p.m., but I was very happy. The late Mr. Henry Clemerson was a kind gentleman and to him I owe a great deal, as you will hear later in my narrative.[1]

I stayed with this firm for twelve months, after which I decided I should like to be apprenticed to the house decorating trade. I was put as an apprentice of Mr. James Hall of Sparrow Hill, Loughborough, being bound for five years, and to work 56½ hours per week at the following rate of pay:

First year	five shillings per week.
Second year	six shillings per week.
Third year	seven shillings per week.
Fourth year	nine shillings per week.
Fifth year	eleven shillings per week.

For any overtime we did (and we did quite a lot in the summer, working 12 hours per day) we received 2d. an hour for the first three years and 3d. an hour for the next two years. Mr. Hall was a very good tradesman and he trained some good men. He was not a bad master and he saw we carried out our apprenticeship agreement and in this way we learnt our trade. We used to do a lot of work in the surrounding villages. Bicycles were only just coming into use; there were no motors or buses — only carrier's carts. If the distance to the village where we were working was under four miles, we used to walk there in the master's time, carrying what material we could, and we walked home at night in our own time. If the distance was over four miles we were required to lodge in the village and an allowance of 6d. per night was made. I remember lodging at Queniborough, Shepshed, Costock, Wymeswold, Long Whatton, Kegworth, Whitwick and other villages. I wonder what boys would think of these conditions today. I do not remember looking upon these conditions as a hardship; indeed there seemed to be much less grumbling and discontent than there is today. I am pleased that working conditions have been improved, as undoubtedly some of them were very bad. Now we seem in places to be tending towards the other extreme.

I remember seeing the man who claimed to be the last Sir Roger Tichborne. He was accused of fraudulently assuming the title to claim a great fortune and after one of the greatest trials in English history, his name was proved to be Arthur Orten and he was sentenced to 14 years' imprisonment. Many people thought he was the true heir and he was invited to Loughborough to a pigeon shooting match on the Greyhound Football ground, and I remember seeing him there — a very stout man.

The first election I remember took place in 1880 when I was eight years old. The working man in 1880 had no vote but this did not stop him from taking a great interest in the election.[2]

There were three candidates for the two vacancies: Lord John Manners and Colonel Burnaby were put forward for the Tories and Hussey Packe, the squire of Prestwold Hall was nominated to fight for the Liberals. There was great excitement. The Tory candidates took up their quarters at the Bulls Head Hotel, High Street, and all the windows were boarded up. Forty or fifty extra policemen were drafted into the town and fifteen to twenty of them were lined up in front of the Bulls Head Hotel. Crowds of people were outside and many ugly rushes and fights took place. Hussey Packe took up his quarters at the King's Head Hotel at the other end of High Street.

Both Tory candidates were returned but Colonel Burnaby died within a year or two of his election and Major Curzon of Woodhouse, heir to the Beaumanor Estate was elected unopposed, in his place. W.E. Gladstone was Prime Minister, and before the next election in 1885, the Third Reform Act[3] was passed giving the working man the vote. While this bill was going through parliament there was great excitement throughout the country as the House of Lords rejected it. Some people thought there would be a revolution. There was a great demonstration held in Loughborough in the Island House Park where Queen's Park, Granby Street, and Packe Street now are, and contingents came from all the country villages with bands and banners. The Lords at last gave way and the bill was passed together with a redistribution of seats. Loughborough returning one member instead of two. The 1885 election brought about a change. For the first time in history, Loughborough returned a Liberal. The candidates were Major Curzon, Tory, and Mr. Johnson-Ferguson, Liberal, the latter being returned by 1040 majority over his Tory opponent. However the government had to appeal to the country in 1886 and Johnson Ferguson was defeated by Mr. Edwin De Lisle by 135 votes. At the next election in 1892 Johnson Ferguson again contested the seat this time beating Edwin Delisle by over 700 votes.

Local sanitation and water supply were very bad at this time. Many houses in Loughborough had only pump water; privies or middens with open ash pits were the only sanitary accommodation. Much of this filth percolated into the drinking water. Very few houses had baths, and the only baths available for people who had not their own, were in four wooden cubicles behind the White Horse Inn, Victoria Street. The privies or middens were mostly emptied at night time and the sewage carted away to some farmland where it polluted the air for a quarter of a mile radius. The old Local Board was alive to the evils of bad sanitation and was doing all it could to obtain more authority to deal with these evils, but lack of water was the chief hindrance to any improvement. In 1884 a calamity threatened the town with a water famine. Nanpantan reservoir was quite empty, so a temporary supply was hurriedly prepared on Derby Road by the railway station, and water was pumped into the pipes from the Burleigh brook. There was strict rationing, and a water famine was averted. George Hodson was the engineer who carried out this work and the town is indebted to him for what he did. We are also indebted to him for his efforts in helping the town to secure the water supply of the Blackbrook which freed the town from the fear of a future scarcity of water.

The Local Board was now petitioning the government to grant a Borough Charter to the town, but it was not until 1888 that the petition was granted. The first municipal election took place on November 1st 1888. I well remember the great excitement and party bitterness shown in the election. I think it was an unfortunate mistake that the new borough introduced party politics into its administration. The result of the election was the return of six Conservatives for Burton Ward, six Liberals for Hastings Ward, four Liberals and two Conservatives for Storer Ward. Thus the Liberals had a majority of two on the first Council. The Liberals elected Joseph Griggs as the first Mayor and packed the council with six Liberal aldermen.

In 1887 the whole country celebrated the Queen's Jubilee. Loughborough certainly did well. All the schoolchildren in the town of every denomination marched into the Market Place from their different schools. Each school entered a competition for the best tableau. It was a wonderful sight with bands playing and flags flying. Policemen, firemen, volunteers and children all marched in procession to Island House Park where tea was provided for the children and the old folk. A grand display of fireworks and games completed the day. Island House Park was bought by subscriptions from the citizens and was presented to the Town Council and was renamed Queen's Park in commemoration of the event.

Events which affected the welfare of the town

There was a great hosiery strike at the Nottingham Manufacturing Company, which lasted for months. A great number of men were imported into the town who were described as blacklegs or strikebreakers. The feeling amongst the workpeople of the town was extremely strong and bitter. In fact, imported men dared not walk about the town. Those few who got lodgings in the town found their houses were surrounded by mobs of angry workers. Windows were smashed and police were detailed to watch these lodgings. The majority of the men who came from places as far off as Heanor and Nottingham were lodged in the factory itself and beds and provisions were provided for them. Stronger forces of police had to be drafted into the town and every weekend they accompanied the workmen to the Midland

Station and met them again on Monday morning; about five or six hundred people followed booing and throwing missiles. It was rare fun for us boys who joined in the crowd although we didn't understand much of the trouble. This strike had a very serious effect on the town and the results were felt for several years. The strikers eventually had to give in but a great number were never given back their jobs. Many families were ruined, many of the men were sent to long terms of imprisonment for acts of violence, and many of the families emigrated to America. Most of these emigrants went to Philadelphia which became the centre of hosiery manufacturing in America, and was able to compete with the English markets, so causing a trade boomerang. As in all fights and strikes the victors and losers suffered alike.

Then in 1887 the Nottingham Manufacturing Company was burnt down to the ground. I was working at Southfield Road at this time. At about 2 p.m. it was rumoured that the Company factory was on fire. I went to look at it and just then only some smoke could be seen coming from the two turrets, but soon the top storey was alight. The fire brigades were summoned from Leicester and round about but they were of little use as the water pressure was not strong enough to reach the top storeys. Soon the top floor gave way and the machinery fell onto the next floor. The same thing happened again until the whole building was a raging furnace. Nothing remained but the bare walls. It took several weeks to clear away the debris, but before it was all cleared away, the March winds came and blew down the walls killing one or two workmen and injuring another.

Army movements

When the government wished to move the different regiments from one part of the country to another, the men did not go by train as now, but by road with all their equipment. Officers used to come several days beforehand, and fix up billets for the men at different inns. If it was a horse regiment they had to find accommodation for men and horses too. All the inn space was taken over and if this was not sufficient they had to provide it elsewhere and none of the townspeople could appeal against this billeting. Sometimes they would stay several days, very often from Friday to Monday or Tuesday. On Sunday they would go to Church. It was a grand sight to see them in their full army dress. Sometimes it would be the Hussars or Coldstream Guards. At other times the Royal Artillery would assemble in the Market Place before marching off to the next town. Officers would then inspect men and horses and if unsatisfactory the offenders would be punished by having to walk beside their horses instead of riding. I have seen many soldiers who for some fault have been strapped to the saddle of a horse and forced to walk or trot beside the horse.[4]

The Royal Artillery used to limber their guns in Devonshire Square, and we used to watch them clean and polish till everything about them shone even to the last button or buckle. That is where the old saying comes in about spit and polish. It was a wonderful sight when two or three hundred horses lined up in the Market Place. The horses understood the orders and bugle sounds as much as the men and each would fall into its proper place, their tails and manes brushed and combed. The whole regiment would then march out in double file through the town on the next stage of their journey.

Sport and Entertainment

Social and other entertainment in Loughborough was always to the fore with sport much more so than it is today. Loughborough Town had two good cricket clubs — Cartwright and Warners and the Nottingham Manufacturing Company — two excellent clubs. There were some outstanding cricketers amongst the Cartwright family, and for the N.M.C. there were Mr. A. Hallam and Mr. Wm. Hallam, who later became a professional bowler. Hathern Village which is included within the Loughborough boundary had a very strong cricket team, and many of their men played for the County.

The town ran a very strong football team too, and there was keen competition between Loughborough and the Leicester Fosse team. Loughborough usually succeeded in carrying off victory. One year Loughborough reached the top of the Midland League and was elevated into the Second Division. It also reached the semi final of the Birmingham Cup beating Birmingham Small Heath and Aston Villa. But the club was unable to meet the heavy expenses involved in Second Division football and the team gradually weakened, but there was still grand football to be seen, and Loughborough was certainly quite a name in football circles then.

Loughborough also boasted two excellent Brass Bands which won several contests. There were two annual events which were well patronised. One was the Loughborough Flower and Fruit show, which was well known all over the Midlands. Special trains were run from Leicester, Nottingham, Derby and other places to Loughborough. Most of the local works closed down for the day or half day. The show was held on Elms Park, which was owned by Mr. E. Warner. Loughborough was second if not equal to the Abbey Park Flower Show in Leicester. There were many prizes for the best display of flowers, fruit and vegetables, which were competed for by people from all over the Midlands, but Loughborough at that time could boast of more allotments than any other place of its size, and working men took a great pride in their allotments and a large number used to exhibit their produce at the various shows. The show usually finished with a balloon ascent, brass band contest and firework display. Now there are only a few enthusiastic exhibitors but not enough to fill one room of the Town Hall.

The annual Agricultural Show was a much larger show than the present one. This was held on Southfield Park and was one of the great events of the year. It was well patronised by visitors from the surrounding villages. At night a display of fireworks together with dancing finished off the show.

The only other entertainment we had was a Christmas Concert at the Baxter Gate Chapel; this was an annual event for over fifty years. The Chapel seated over 1250 and every seat was filled. After the concert a good supper was provided and enormous quantities of beef, ham, and other good things were consumed. It is now over fifty years since this concert was discontinued because of lack of support.

Most of our other entertainment was provided by the different churches in the town. I think that is why the old people have such a love for the place where they worshipped in their younger days as they remember the good times and happy fellowship they enjoyed together.

At Whitsuntide each year there were interesting functions. On Whit Monday all the Friendly Societies used to walk in procession through the town dressed in the costume of their order and headed by a brass band. They went to the Greyhound Athletic Ground where sports were held. These sports attracted competitors from all over the country. The next day, the Loughborough Football Club held its annual sports. In fact the town used to make a general holiday of these two days of sports.

Some good circuses came to Loughborough in the course of the year and they used to parade through the town. I well remember Barnum and Bailey's great American Show coming. It was a fascinating show and one that I shall remember all my life.

Footnotes

1.   The author's younger brother Albert was also to work for Clemersons and became a director of the firm.

2.   This was not entirely accurate, as the 1867 Reform Act had enfranchised those working men in the towns who paid rates or who paid £10 rent a year.

3.   The Third Reform Bill of 1884 was made up of two parts which complemented each other — The Reform Act and the Redistribution Act. The Reform Act extended the vote to householders and £10 lodgers in the counties. The Redistribution Act deprived some 79 towns of less than 15,000 population of their representation in Parliament and towns between 15,000 and 50,000 were to have one M.P. only.

4.   The author's wife's grandfather, Samuel Sutton, who had fought at Waterloo, had suffered this punishment.

3.   The Shepherd Family, c. 1898. From the top left to right: Caroline, Arthur, John. In front, from left to right: Albert, John (father), Amy (mother), Sarah. Absent: William and Frederick who had emigrated to America.

Chapter 3

1893 - 1913
Business and Family Man

I had now completed my apprenticeship but being October it was a very bad time of the year for getting work. It was not unusual for a painter to be out of work for six or seven weeks during the winter months. My master had always told me that I should have no difficulty in getting a job, but the last day of my apprenticeship came and no mention had been made to me about staying with him. I went to him for my indentures and asked him what he wished me to do if he expected me to start work as a journeyman. We had a little argument about the wage I required. He suggested that I should take 6d. per hour until the spring and then receive the standard rate. To this I would not agree. I told him I should require the standard rate of 6½d. per hour, at once. Eventually he agreed to this.

During that winter we were out of work for six weeks because of bad frosty weather. The next summer the standard wage was increased to 7d. an hour. We were very busy all summer and were able to put in many hours overtime, working from 6 a.m. until 8 p.m. The following winter I was out of work for five weeks. We were pleased to get a job however small and I was sent to Hathern Rectory to limewash a pantry and dairy place. I had to push a handcart there and back with plank and tressels and material for the job but I finished the work in one day and returned by 7 p.m. One of the men who had no work saw me. I think he must have felt jealous, because he walked with me a little way and told me he was hard up. I said how sorry I was for him and as I was single and he was married I gave him

4. Arthur Shepherd, 1896.

2/6d. which was about half my earnings for the day's work. After putting away my scaffolding and materials I went to the front of the shop to enquire if I was wanted for work next day. My master said he could find me a little work at some of his own houses. He also said the man to whom I had just given 2/6d. was prepared to work until the spring at a 1d. less than I was being paid. If I was willing to accept the same I could come to work on the morrow. I declined the offer. I had always had a great respect for my master although he was hard and grudging over money, but I lost that respect from then on. To find work I went round to other painting firms in town, but to no avail. I managed to do a little work on my own, after which Mr. Wm. Bass of Church Gate employed me to decorate the Free Wesleyan

Chapel in Woodgate. I stayed with Mr. Bass, who was a good master, until July when he was unable to find further work for me. Again I visited all the painting firms, with no success. I heard that Nanpantan Hall the residence of E. Paget Esq. was being painted, so I walked to the Hall but no more painters were required. I now decided to get some work on my own account and I was successful in making a contract to paint and decorate some newly built houses at a low price. This made me decide to start on my own account as a painter, paperhanger and house decorator.

I had only about £20 capital but I got a sign written and fixed over my father's house in Freehold Street. Thus in July 1894 I became a Master Painter and Decorator. If I had persistently been unable to find work I had seriously contemplated emigrating to America, where my elder brother already was, but I was fortunately kept busy throughout the summer. I soon found I was seriously handicapped by lack of room and a workshop. I went to Derby to Joseph Mason and Company, one of the most reliable paint manufacturers in the country. I put my case to them, told them all the capital I had and what material I required. Evidently they were satisfied with my candid statement and agreed to let me have any material I required. Our firm is still trading with this Company after fifty eight years and the relations between us have always been most pleasant.

A small shop on Nottingham Road became vacant, with living accommodation, and I got the tenancy from Messrs. Wolley and Holbeach at an inclusive rent of 4/7d. per week. In addition I was able to rent a suitable workshop at the rear with a good yard and draw in gateway.

This was one of the great decisions of my life; it was a great business undertaking but it also meant that I must get married. On October 20th 1894 I was married at Baxter Gate Chapel, by the late Rev. R.F. Handford, to one of the best women that God gave to man. I say this in all sincerity and I thank God for bestowing this great blessing on me. Whatever prosperity has come to me has come through her loving help and loyalty through the many years we have been together. Many have been the trials we have faced together. Looking back over the past years, I sometimes wonder how she was able to do all the work which was required in attending to the shop, while I was away at work, and in bringing up a large family with very little outside help. In the early days I had very little capital, but we were both determined not to run into debt. We procured several pieces of furniture at various sales before we were married but as I had only £25 to spend on my home, we had to spend it with the greatest of care. Our small house had only two bedrooms, one of which we used as a sitting room, so with useful wedding presents we soon made ourselves comfortable.

I mentioned earlier that Alderman Clemerson was one of my best friends. I went to see him and explained my circumstances to him. He immediately sent his manager down to advise me about the best selling lines and instructed him to let me have whatever I required on sale or return. We became close friends and worked together on many committees in later years, when we were both serving on the Town Council. I believe that he was one of the most useful and far-seeing Councillors the town ever had. He was I think the last Mayor to serve the town without remuneration. Since then the Mayors have all received a salary to help meet expenses. Whether this change has been for the good of the town is open to argument.

There was plenty of work coming in to keep me fully employed, and I was very busy at nights preparing materials for the next day's work or dressing the shop window. It was usually 10 p.m. before I had finished work.

Christmas 1894 was a lovely day, the sun was shining and there was just a little frost. On Boxing Day a dense fog descended and this continued for two or three days. Then there was a keen frost which continued for over thirteen weeks, right into March 1895. The river Soar and the canal were frozen hard. The skaters had a splendid time; it was possible to skate from Loughborough to London. The ice got so thick that you could take a horse and cart over the Soar or the canal without any danger. Stalls with hot refreshments were on the ice daily, but this was the pleasant side of the picture; there was also a tragic and distressing side.

All building work stopped and many other trades were brought to a complete standstill. There was no dole in those days, but a relief fund was opened for the poor and needy. Shops in different parts of the town were opened to serve soup and free meals to those in desperate need. The water pipes were frozen under the ground and men from the water department were sent round every day to open the main water pipes in the road. A bell was rung and people came out to fill their buckets with water for the next day. This severe frost went on right through the winter until March. The 'Great Frost' of 1895 is still remembered. In 1896 the frost was also very keen but not so prolonged.

This weather hit us very hard as it came only three months after we were married, when we had scarcely got our shop and business going. For thirteen weeks I could not earn a penny and all we had to live on was what came from sales in the shop. But sales were very low because the people round the Nottingham Road district were very poor. Many times our dinner consisted of 2d. worth of white herring with potatoes.

Only once did my wife break down and that was when we only had one half penny left in the till after we had paid for the lamp oil which we had sold and found that we had to pay cash on delivery for more. I drew out the balance in my Post Office Account which amounted to 1/9d. It was some time before I was able to work again at my trade because the frost was in the walls and ice was about for some weeks after the frost had gone. The ice was so thick on the canal that the water had to be run off from under the ice. Then the ice broke off in great blocks and floated down through the locks to the river.

The Gt. Central Railway was being built during 1895 and a number of houses, some newly built, and several streets had to be destroyed round the Moor Lane district, to make room for the new station. This gave work to some of the men unemployed through the severe frost.

1895 had its bright side. On October 27th my wife presented me with a daughter; it was grand to come home from work to be welcomed by the smile of a baby girl. On February 1st 1899 my first boy was born and on October 26th 1900 my second daughter was born.

Conditions were changing; the new Town Council, elected on November 1st 1888, had set about remedying some of the evils. Where water was available the old pumps were being condemned and town water was laid on and water closets were installed. Many people had baths put in their houses, although only cold water was laid on. Newly built houses for the better class had bathrooms with hot and cold water laid on. Gas began to replace candles and oil lamps in many homes. Gas was also used for street lighting, and the lamp lighter, with his ladder, lit the burners at night and returned in the morning to turn them out. The safety bicycle, with its hard rubber tyres, enabled workers to get into the country after working hours.

One morning as I was going to work about 7 o' clock, I saw a policeman running about in the gardens, where now stands Oliver Road. A man came out of the gardens and gave himself up to the policeman. The man wanted to go down Burton Street but the policeman insisted on taking him up Park Road. I knew the man quite well; he was an ex-Sergeant Major who kept a little shop at the corner of South Street and Woodgate. He was also caretaker at the Philharmonic Hall. I did not know, when I saw him arrested, what crime he had committed but it appeared that he had killed his wife that morning after finding her with another man. He was found guilty and hanged. I think it was a shame. In normal circumstances he was a quiet, sober and respectable man.

In 1899 war broke out in South Africa between Britain and the Boers. Everyone expected it to be over in a few months. Volunteers came forward from all over the country hoping they would be sent out before it was over. However the country was ill prepared for war and the people soon began to realise that it was quite easy to start a war but not so easy to finish it. We were in for a great many surprises.

I well remember the Leicestershire Cavalry marching by our shop on Nottingham Road, with crowds of people cheering them. They were a smart lot of young fellows. I am sorry to say that very few marched back past my shop. They were in the first engagement at the hill called Spion Cop and most of them were shot down. The Boers finally surrendered in 1902 but not until many thousands of lives were lost. There was great rejoicing when it was over, but the most exciting time was when Mafeking was relieved. The people seemed to go crazy, quite respectable people did the most unusual things. Fires were started in the market place and when the firemen came to put out the flames they cut the hosepipes. One of our present freemen of the Borough had to appear before the magistrates on a charge of cutting the hosepipe and obstructing the police. These outbursts of patriotism were not confined to Loughborough and even now if anything silly takes place it is said that people have gone maffiking.

On January 22 1901 Queen Victoria died after a reign of sixty three years. In 1902 King Edward VII was crowned with the usual rejoicings and festivities. Now began quite a new age, many customs passing away and what would have shocked society a few years back became quite ordinary.

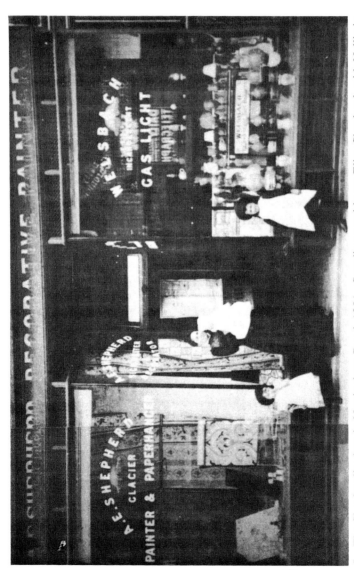

5. The Shepherd's shop in Nottingham Road, 1901. Standing outside are Eliza Shepherd, with Nellie in her arms, Arthur on the left and Lilian on the right. The shop sign is still evident on the side of the building today.

In 1906 a great strike took place at the Brush works and lasted quite a long time; it was very bad for trade in the town and hundreds of houses became empty. Whole rows of houses stood vacant in Falcon St., Morley St., Hartington St. and Ratcliffe Rd.

In 1907 occurred the first death in our family. My youngest sister who had been ill for a long time died at the age of 41 years. In January 1909 my dear mother passed away in her 77th year. She was a dear old soul and a good Christian. When we were all at home, every Sunday evening, before we went to bed she would get us together and offer up a prayer for us all, asking God to watch over us. Unfortunately she was totally blind for the last seven years of her life.

In August 1908, three months before my mother died, my wife presented me with twin boys. 'Not more than we otherwise deserved, but the Lord did give us more.' My mother, although unable to see them, was delighted to have them on her knee. The family now consisted of four boys and two girls. One of the twins, William, took dangerously ill with bronchitis when he was two months old. Dr. Corcoran visited him every day for two weeks and when the bill came it was only £2.

I was now established in business and was earning a comfortable living. I had built and removed to more convenient premises on the Nottingham Road at the corner of Queens Road, which had just been opened. Queens Road provided a kind of bypass for those travelling from Nottingham to Leicester, so that they could avoid the narrow Baxter Gate. I secured several large painting contracts and was employing quite a large number of workmen.

In 1911 I was elected by the burgesses of the Hastings Ward to serve on the Council. This meant a lot of extra work, often having to neglect my business. By being a councillor you gain a lot of valuable experience; it also broadens your mind and if you are determined to do your duty to the electors you must be prepared to make great sacrifices, very often receiving more kicks than thanks for your trouble. I was elected onto several committees and have attended as many as 300 meetings in a year. I served on the Council for ten years.

In 1913 I was asked if I would undertake the catering and running of the poor children's breakfast on Christmas morning. For the past twenty five years it had been managed by Mr. A. Faulks. Over six hundred poor children were provided with a breakfast. The first year I proceeded on the usual lines but this did not satisfy me as it was not my idea of what a Christmas breakfast should be. I arranged the menu as follows: bread, cut thin, with butter not margarine; over 170 lbs of Lacey's best pork pie, followed by best plum cake with plenty of good tea. On leaving the hall each child was given an orange, mince pie and a bar of Cadbury's Milk Chocolate. In later years Mr. T. Cartwright of Cartwright and Warners provided me with a new sixpenny piece to be given to each child. After Mr. Cartwright's death, Mr. Malcolm Moss stepped into the breach and gave a silver threepenny bit. The company grew until there used to be close on 700 children sit down. I always had a number of willing workers come forward; many of them had sat down at the breakfast in past years. During the whole of the time I ran the breakfast I never asked for a penny towards expenses, but the money always came and the work was done voluntarily. Many people looked upon their subscriptions as a debt which they owed me. The subscribers all received a balance sheet of income and expenses. When I took over the breakfast cost £15 but in the latter years, including the gifts, it cost over £50. It was very hard work for the few days before Christmas and we had to have our own Christmas festivities on Boxing Day. All the books, with the cost of goods and gifts, can be seen at the Loughborough Free Library; they are interesting if only to compare the price of food. I do think the clergy missed a fine opportunity of getting among the poor children. During the whole 25 years I only remember one minister who used to come to the breakfast.

I carried it on for 25 years and was sorry to give it up but the Second World War came along and the tradesmen were unable to supply the food, so there was no alternative. It had become one of Loughborough's Christmas institutions.

I was presented with a framed picture of 'The Good Shepherd' by the Loughborough Education Committee, which I prize highly. The Education Committee decided to make the presentation immediately after the 'Robins Breakfast'. It was a closely guarded secret and it was certainly a surprise to me, but there was also a surprise for the Mayor and the Committee because the picture could not be found. It turned out that the caretaker had locked it in the offices and gone out for Christmas Day. So they made the presentation without the present. It was all very amusing but the present came later during the week.

6. Robin's Breakfast, c. 1920.

Chapter 4

1914 - 1918
The Great War

The year 1914 began all bright and pointed towards the country being very prosperous. Trade was good and the standard of living was rising. Loughborough was recovering from the Brush Strike and trade generally in the town was very good. I had several small speculations in land and house property which proved successful. In July I was offered, by Mr. Arthur Ball of Nottingham, the remaining portions of the Elms Park estate at a very low price. The laying out of the estate had not proved remunerative to him and he was prepared to cut his losses. So I agreed to buy all the unsold plots. Not being able to finance the whole scheme myself, I persuaded Mr. Walter Coltman to join with me. On July 20 I signed the contract and paid a deposit. Then suddenly, like a bolt from the blue, came the Great War. On August 4th war was declared with Germany. All trade for a time came to a standstill. Men threw over their jobs and rushed to join the forces. Our trade was one that was not considered essential. Up to this time I had always taken as my motto 'hope for the best and prepare for the worst'; I had certainly not prepared for this. All sales of land were stopped and the Council commandeered all vacant plots of land, paying nothing for them, but they did not relieve me of my liabilities to pay interest on the money I had borrowed. I was about at my wits end to know what was best for me to do. However difficulties are made to be overcome and by working almost night and day I managed to keep my head above water.

On January 13 1916, I was in my shop packing a parcel for my daughter Nellie's fiancé, Wilfred Cross, who was serving in

Salonika, when my eldest son Arthur came in. He said that it was rumoured that the Zeppelins had come as far as Leicester. There had been much talk but it was thought impossible for them to reach the Midlands. Then, all at once came two explosions which shook the house, followed a few minutes later by another two. Two bombs were dropped on the Empress works, smashing the roof and killing six people. My youngest daughter, Lilian, was working at the Empress works as a tracer. It was the first time she had been asked to work overtime.

I went to the works to find the roads were strewn with glass and twisted telephone wires. I could get no information from anyone. All kinds of rumours were spread as to the number of people killed. Men and women were panicking, running into the fields. I went round the different groups trying to find my daughter. I returned home but she was not there; however my cellar was filled with people seeking shelter. I went back to the works and again returned home with no news but this time she was at home. The management had gathered the young girls together in the basement until the raid was over and then one of the staff escorted them home. Apparently she had been blown through the swing doors by the blast but fortunately was unhurt.

Two bombs were also dropped by the Gas Works, one in the Crown and Cushion Yard and another in the Rushes, killing a man and his wife. They had been married only a few weeks. Also a Mrs. Adcock, a brushmaker's wife, was killed. My youngest brother was going home to Knighthorpe at the time, and saw these people killed. As I stood at the door of my shop, I saw the Zeppelin drop two more bombs over in the direction of the Sewage Farm. Many people doubted this because no bombs were found, but I believed my own eyes. Several years later when the canal was being drained and a large sewer pipe was being laid under the canal from Lower Cambridge Street, a bomb was found in the canal.

7.   Arthur Shepherd and family, 1916. From the top left: Arthur, Lilian, Nellie, Albert (in the centre), Arthur, John, William, Eliza.

8. Army assembles in the Market Place, 1914.

Until this air raid, no precautions had been taken. There is no doubt that it was the lights which attracted the Zeppelin — the Empress works were ablaze with lights, and a theatre on Ashby Road was also lit.

Special precautions were now taken against any surprise attack. Squads of volunteers were posted in different parts of the town; my premises were used for the Nottingham Road end of the town.

On April 24 1916, I lost my dear father. For many years he had suffered from creeping paralysis. He was 82 and although helpless in body, his mind was alert. He had lived a quiet, sober, steady life. He was a splendid father and I can repeat what was said of Barnabas that 'he was a good man'.

The war continued. My eldest son joined the A.F.C. the day he was eighteen. I had to join the Civil Defence Force. We used to drill in the market place and then we were marched off to guard the Brush Works for the night. Then I was called up for service and passed A1 at the age of 46. I applied to a tribunal and was given four months exemption to dispose of or close my business.

One day we received a telegram from the War Office with a prepaid railway fare for my wife and I to go to Somerville Hospital, Oxford to see my son who had collapsed with double pneumonia and was dangerously ill. We set out that night in pouring rain. My wife's dress was soaked and the train was very cold. We arrived at Oxford at about 3 a.m. and there was no fire at the hospital, nor any coal to make one. That was the state of the country in 1918. Fortunately my son made a satisfactory recovery.

In August 1918 I was working at the Empress works limewashing the walls. As I was climbing off the gantry rail on to the ladder I missed my footing on the stave and fell from a height of about eighteen feet onto some iron melting pots. I thought my back was broken. The ambulance took me home and I was carried in a sheet to my bed and was unable to move for several days. Although the doctor gave little hope of my recovery, my back was not broken and after a few days I recovered from the shock and I gradually grew stronger. But there was one immediate result — it wiped out any possibility of an army career for me! During the time I was recovering peace was declared.

It was a long time before I was able to do any work. This accident made a great difference to my life, for I determined that whatever happened I would take life a little more easily. I gave up my shop in Nottingham Road and bought the house called 'Charnwood' at the corner of Park Road and Forest Road. This is the house from which I used to fetch the skimmed milk as a boy. I carried on my business as a painter and decorator from this private house. As my business had been long established my customers followed me. My wife and I together with our now grown up family spent fifteen years of happy family life at 'Charnwood'.

Chapter 5

1918 - 1939
Property Development

I decided to devote more time to the building of houses and the development of land. There were any number of bargains to be made and if I had had more capital I could have made a fortune. I entered into a kind of partnership with Walter Mountney, a man after my own heart. We opened a joint account and borrowed money from the bank, depositing all deeds as security. Despite no legal agreement, we were together for over twenty five years without a word of disagreement. We were developing the town at the same time as developing our own estates. We received very little encouragement from the different authorities with which we had to deal. Loughborough in 1918 was very confined and cramped and only extended as far as the Woodbrook on the Forest Road. We decided to develop the town in the Forest Road and Loughborough Road areas. All the land was held by the large landowners, who refused to sell. We were asked to join a small syndicate to develop the Burleigh Estate, which comprised over six hundred acres on the Forest side of the town, stretching as far as Nanpantan and up to Snells Nook on Ashby Road. After two years of negotiation the sale was effected. It was decided to put up for sale the whole estate in lots. A reserve price was fixed and any member of the syndicate who wished to buy could do so. We bought about fifty acres and soon wished we had purchased more, as there was a great demand for allotments. We bought back several fields from some purchasers, giving them a handsome profit. The land was cut up into suitable plots and roads were planned so that the land could be used for building plots. These plots were sold at prices varying from 9d. to 1/3d. per yard according to position. Most were bought on the instalment system, £3 deposit and 10/- per month. Over a thousand plots were sold off and I believe a good profit was made on them, whenever they were resold. After the Burleigh Estate had been sold, E.H. Warner of Quorn Hall decided to sell his estate, and offered his tenants the first option of purchasing their farms. Mr. George Levers who had purchased his farm sold to me at a substantial profit and we were able to proceed with our development.

Up to this time the only way to get to Beacon Road and Herrick Road was to come down to Park Road corner. We now started, at a cost of £6,000, to make Outwoods Drive, replacing the cart track which went to the farms. Despite the shortage of houses the authorities put all possible obstacles in our way. Before we could persuade them to lay water, gas or electricity we had to guarantee them 10% on the outlay for so many years. Actually we carried the whole burden of these services for some years. The houses did not sell quickly because of lack of transport to the town. There was soon an outcry from the public for Beacon Road to be made a public highway fit for vehicles to travel on. The Council decided to make up the road, but it still took a long time to fully develop Outwoods Drive. There was an increasing demand for building plots on Forest Road and Ashby Road areas.

One day I had occasion to visit my daughter who was living in Derby. I went round the outskirts of the town to see where they were building, and I noticed some land was for sale. I went to the sale, where the lot in question — a field of about 4 or 5 acres — did not reach its reserved price. I asked what the reserve price was, consulted my partner and we bought it. We immediately started to develop it and the plots were sold before we had time to finish the roads. We and two other gentlemen bought an adjoining farm and submitted a layout plan to the Derby Council, which gave its approval, advice and assistance.

Both the Gas and Electricity Committees wrote to ask our permission to lay gas mains and electricity cables, and water mains were also laid down. We could not understand this treatment which was so different from the way we were hindered by the Loughborough Council.

I had now served on the Council for ten years but owing to my many interests, some of which clashed with my council work, I decided not to seek re-election. During the time I was on the Council, I was instrumental in making several improvements to the town. One was the securing of the property where now stands the Post Office. It came to my knowledge that my partner and another gentleman had bought the big house and grounds which belonged to Mr. Craddock. This property was the key to the opening up of great improvements to the town. The property ran alongside a passage known as Conery Passage; this was about six feet wide and ran from Nottingham Road to Baxter Gate. There had been many disagreements on the Council about purchasing this property; the project to join Baxter Gate to Nottingham Road had always been defeated because of the cost. I was Vice Chairman of the Highways' Committee at the time and I secured an option on the house at a very low price. This was on the Saturday. I telephoned the Chairman Ald. R.J. Clifford and when I mentioned the price, he asked me on no account to let it pass. The Highways' Committee met on the Monday and decided to purchase the property. Before the news leaked out all the Committee were sworn to secrecy. It was about the only time I remember a secret being kept on the Council. As I had an option on the big house and grounds it was left in my hands to try and purchase the remaining property. The Committee arranged to meet on the following Friday. There were thirteen houses which we wanted to purchase and I knew that most of them had been withdrawn from sale because they did not reach their reserve. I also knew that some members of the Council were interested in this

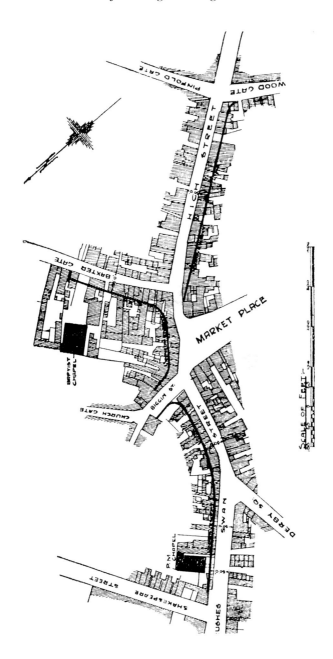

9. Proposed street widening in Loughborough. The sketch, published in the Loughborough Echo on October 25th, 1923, was a rough copy of what was submitted by the Loughborough Town Council for the approval of the Government authorities.

property. Before Friday I had secured all this property either by paying a deposit or getting an option. The Council was very pleased and asked me to negotiate for the remaining twelve houses in Craddock Street and three more in Freehold Street. Within the next seven days I got contracts for the purchase of twelve houses. For the other three I had to pay a higher price as the owner got some clue as to what was going on. The Committee was now able to recommend to the Council that it should purchase all this property — only leaving the Royal George Inn and two adjoining cottages. All this for under £6,000. I am not wishing to boast but I estimate that I saved the Council between five and six thousand pounds. A special vote of thanks was passed by the Council to be recorded in their minutes.

I still feel that if all my suggestions had been carried out the town would have further benefitted. When the widening of the High Street was under construction, I proposed that it should be sixty feet wide but the Surveyor opposed it. He said fifty feet was ample. I replied that in twenty five years' time the problem of congestion would be as bad as it was at that time. Who was right? In Baxter Gate I won my case for fifty feet instead of the proposed forty feet. When the Nottingham Road Primitive Methodists pulled down some shops adjoining the chapel, I proposed that the line be brought back to the line of the chapel with suitable compensation being paid. This would ultimately have widened Nottingham Road as far as Clarence Street by five feet. Now, owing to the narrow neck between Queens Road and Clarence Road it is a danger spot when the work people are coming home at meal times.

Once while I was a member of the Council I had a very embarrassing time. It came to our knowledge that the owners of the property at the bottom of Baxter Gate and High Street were willing to sell. T.B. Garton negotiated on our behalf and after some months we made a final offer with a time limit for acceptance. After the Council meeting on the following Monday we were asked to go into Committee. The Council was pledged to secrecy and the Town Clerk read a letter he had received from Moss and Taylor acting on behalf of Mr. McCurdy offering this property to the Council. It stated that they had had another offer for the property but wished the town to have the opportunity of purchasing it. A small sub-committee was formed and I was chosen to serve on it. I immediately told my partner and under the circumstances we felt honour bound to withdraw our offer and leave the Council free to negotiate. Eventually the Council turned down the offer, yet a few years later paid £4,000 more than if they had accepted the offer at the time. Had I not been on the Council and free to buy I would have made at least £4,000 profit.

The old proverb that you cannot serve two masters was clearly demonstrated. Although there would have been nothing dishonourable if we had bought the property, as we were negotiating long before it was offered to the Council, I thought it would be indiscreet of me as a Councillor. It was many years before any one knew that we were the people who had been trying to buy the property. I now finished my association with the Council and was free to speculate as I liked.

In 1926 Mr. Edgar Corah, the owner of Wm. Corah & Son Ltd. Builders and Contractors died. I had long contemplated starting a company of builders and decorators. My own business as a decorator was well established and I had one son in partnership. My third son had just ended his time as a bricklayers apprentice and my eldest son had been sent to a firm of builders at Derby. When the firm of Wm. Corah & Son came on the market I approached the Executors and bought shares in this firm which had been established in 1851.

We bought back thirty five acres of the Burleigh estate in Loughborough and opened up Fairmount Drive, Holywell Drive, Benscliffe Drive, Highfield Drive and Shepherds Close.

We also opened up Park Road and Parkfields Drive. We found a ready sale for houses. We also owned some old cottages in Mill Street, now renamed Market Street, which we wanted to pull down as they were not fit for human habitation. We tried to get a closing order but the Council would not agree. The Sanitary Inspector, Mr. Binscliffe did his utmost to have them demolished, but it took some time to get this passed and then it was only carried by one vote. We cleared out one of the worst slum areas in the centre of the town. We carried out one of the best street improvements in the town without incurring the cost of a penny to the town.

In 1938 my partner and I bought a very old residence in Wards End named Atherstone House. This we pulled down and in its place erected a block of buildings including the set of offices occupied by the Inland Revenue. These offices were built to the specification of the Ministry of Works. We built three lock up shops underneath the offices. Here is another great improvement in the centre of the town.

On a more personal note, in 1937 my wife and I had a memorable trip to the United States and Canada to visit my brothers, William and Frederick, who had lived in Philadelphia for nearly fifty years.

In 1939 we suffered the loss of our second son Albert who died after an operation for appendicitis. Up to this time I was one of the happiest men in Loughborough, having four sons and two daughters with their children all growing up and all my children were strong and healthy. My son appeared to make a good recovery after his operation when suddenly complications set in and he had to undergo a further operation. After four days his heart suddenly weakened and he died at the age of 35 years. It was a great shock to us all. He was a grand boy and it seems a shame for him to be taken just in the prime of life. There is a saying that time will heal all things. I have not found it so. It is now 15 years since we lost him and few days pass without something happening to bring his memory before us.

Chapter 6

1939 - 1952
War and its Aftermath

In September 1939 the Second World War started and once again our business was brought to a standstill. All businesses not essential to the war effort were stopped and the country's entire effort was turned towards the production of weapons and material for war. Many men who were called up had to sell their businesses. We could do nothing in our trade. Terrible days were ahead. Bombs were dropping all round us and shelters had to be erected hurriedly all over the country. All sales of land were stopped and even houses we had begun to build had to be left. In February 1943 Mr. Mounteney, my partner in land development, died after a short illness. He was a man who was very much missed for I know he had helped many tradesmen in times of difficulty.

In the same year I was unfortunately taken ill and had a serious operation to remove a growth from my intestine. Dr. Goode told me that I was one in a thousand to get over such an operation and make such a good recovery. I was unable to do work of any kind for the next twelve months.

After the war, there was a great shortage of houses and everyone in the building trade thought they were in for a boom. But alas the new Labour Government introduced what they called planning. They brought in the Act fixing the sale of land, which no one could understand. Permits had to be obtained for everything that was used; whole armies of officials, called the Land Board, were appointed and the whole business was thrown into chaos. Previously we could submit plans to the Council and were able to start building within a week; now we had to waste anything up to six or nine months before permission to build was given. We had land fully developed ready for houses to be built but were greatly handicapped by the regulations. I was told by solicitors that it was the most idiotic bill that had ever been put on the statute book. At the present time the government has intimated that a new bill will be brought before the next session of parliament to amend and improve the present Act. I am anxiously looking forward to see what will happen.

We were hindered in many other ways; officials came and took stock of all our timber and we had to sell it to the government at a fixed price. Then it was sold back to us at very nearly double the price. A great part of our staff's time is taken up filling in forms and trying to get permits for the most simple of jobs. We have been harassed in every possible way by officials who know nothing of the trade. All this adds to the costs.

10. Arthur and Eliza Shepherd on their Golden Wedding Anniversary, 1944.

Another difficulty is added in the form of development charges. All the solicitors I have consulted say they are unable to advise the best action to take. Officials can make what charge they think fit. I have sold five or six plots of land all adjoining one another and the development charge has varied from £250 to £435 a plot. Such heavy charges have brought the development of building land to a standstill and private enterprise is being killed.

On October 20 1944 my wife and I celebrated our Golden Wedding. We had had a very happy fifty years. Although we had a very hard struggle in our early days, it was a great pleasure working together for the benefit of our children and watching them grow into good and useful citizens.

In May 1951 I had a pain in my thigh and it was on one of my visits to the doctor's surgery that I tripped going into the waiting room and my thigh was broken right across. I was sent to Harlow Wood Orthopaedic Hospital and was there for over five months. It was while there that I decided to write my memoirs. I am pleased to say that I have made and am still making a very good recovery. I did not expect to be able to walk again as I do.

I thank God for His mercies in giving me health and strength again. It is now eleven months since I had my accident and my wife and I have celebrated our 80th birthdays. Last week we had our 58th wedding anniversary. We are looking forward to and pray that God will keep us in good health so that we may celebrate our Diamond Wedding in two years' time.[1]

Footnote

1.   Our grandparents duly celebrated their Diamond Wedding. Grandfather died suddenly of a stroke on February 20th 1962, aged 90 years and Grandmother died aged 91 the following year.